RAISED BED

GARDENING

FOR BEGINNERS

TABLE OF CONTENTS

INTRODUCTION

Modernity has taken over, and here and there, by and then, buildings keep sprouting up everywhere, leaving little spaces around for actual gardens and a means to practice horticulture; the art or science of cultivating gardens or a form of small-scale agriculture. Also, with modernity comes impatience and many people prefer to scarf down canned, over-fertilized and processed food all around.

So, you being here means you are part of those who still crave food directly served to you from Mother Nature due to your taste or part of a health condition. Or, you would love to have your own little garden without breaking savings, a garden that stresses you less and also a therapeutic purpose or a coping mechanism from reality.

Then, that comes the question, how do I get started? I literally know nothing about gardening, what to do? Well, here is the good news. With this book, anybody who put their mind and heart in it can create their own successful raised bed gardens. This book contains the steps you need to follow, the tools required, the pest and the weed control; basically all you need to know.

The purpose of this book is to guide you through the concept of raised bed gardening, what you need to know about raised bed gardening, and the advantages of having your own raised bed garden. Alongside, you will be familiarized with the challenges that come with creating a raised bed garden, and the solutions to them will be proffered in details.

Much more things that will be explored in this book are how to know the types of soil suitable for your raised bed garden, how to get them, and how to prepare them. The sites relevant to match your taste to bring up your raised beds will not be left unexplored. The types of vegetables suitable for raised beds and how they are planted, the pests to watch out for, and how they are controlled will be discussed at length in this book. Not to forget the basic and essential equipment needed to start growing your crops in raised beds and the weed control methods. You will be initiated to the idea of it all. The secrets to a high-yielding garden? Check! This book will let you in on the secrets to having a yielding and rewarding raised bed garden.

With this guide, anybody can create their own successful raised bed garden, which includes you. And if you are still having doubts about creating your own raised bed garden, this book is just what you need to get rid of your fear and know that raised bed gardening is much simpler, adventurous, and more fun than you have made it out to be.

CHAPTER 1: ABOUT RAISED BED GARDENING

A raised bed garden means putting the garden created on top of the soil level. It is usually made up of different bodies or frames, which the entirety of it all depends on your choice; it could be wood or plastic of high quality or bricks, and it goes on. The choice of creation depends on you to suit your taste and your style. Usually, the soil in raised bed gardens is confined into three-to-four-foot-wide in the body or frame, which, as said earlier, depends totally on your choice or style and can be any size, shape, or length to your liking.

Raised bed gardening can glance through history's eyes, dating back to the medieval eras where wattle fences are edged with the beds. Fast forward to the 18th century, when the Parisian market gardeners used a whole lot of horse manure to build up plots and have their gardens on them.

Creating your own raised bed garden is pretty easy, and because of the raised soil level, working on the raised bed gardens comes with little stress and decreases the risks of back straining while working on the garden. It is easy to go with your chair or stool and work on your garden without having to bend over the garden and strain your back.

In raised bed gardening, your beds or frames' barriers keep pests away and prevent soil concentration or compaction and make it puffy and fluffy. Also, it provides good drainage and prevents pathway weeds from springing up. Having a raised bed garden is easy, as long as you have the basic knowledge about it and the idea of the essential tools and how they are used. You don't need to break a bank or your savings to create your own raised bed garden, which matches your taste and style. Direct soil is available to raised beds because they have direct contact with the ground, which allows the roots of the plant to go deeper into the ground for the provision of awaiting nutrients.

The concept of raised bed gardening is to grow your vegetables around you and your environment without blowing gardening out of proportion. It allows you to practice small-scale agriculture and horticulture; it is the perfect solution for all lovers of natural food and homemade gardens that come without stress and the extravagance that might come with full-scale gardening.

Raised bed gardening comes with its advantages; it brings nature closer to the lovers of Mother Nature. It brings freshly harvested vegetables to the table, which improves a healthy style of eating. It can also be used as a way for keeping one's mental health in check. It comes with a therapeutic package. Raised bed gardening can also be created as just a hobby and can be very rewarding through the proceeds' sales or just keeping it all up for the family. Either way, it is a win-win situation.

Why You Should Use Raised Beds

1.   Easy to assemble. Building a raised bed garden isn't hard to do and it's even easier if you buy it in a kit form because it involves the sourcing of materials, measuring and cutting to size out of the equation; therefore the kit saves time and limits waste. The raised beds can be built out of wooden, sleepers or corrugated sheeting. The steel raised beds come in a flat package and they don't take long to assemble. They are also long-lasting, durable, strong, and termite resistant.

2.   Making use of raised beds saves you the stress of having to till up your soil from year to year to get fertilizer added. The raised beds can easily be maintained by adding materials such as mulches, manures, compost and other soil materials from the top. The raised beds have a way of getting their tilling done themselves since roots and worms can easily push their way through the soil themselves.

3.   The pathways created by the raised beds make it easier to maintain because of the definitive line between the path and the bed.

4.   Weeding a large area of land can lead to knee and back strain as well as exhausting a large amount of your time.

Making use of the raised beds saves you a lot of stress and the back pain that might come up from bending to weed.

5. Due to the smaller amount of space with which the raised bed garden is built, they are more easily nurtured. This will in turn help with good aeration, reduced soil compaction as well as fewer weeds and pests. Once you have all these, you can be sure of having more vegetation being produced from the raised garden.

6. The raised beds can be created with wire mesh below them so that they can be easily moved around for sunlight. This is also beneficial to crop rotation practice.

7. With less compaction of dirt, your soil will get drained easily. Using the raised beds enables moisture to move around and get drained when the needs arise. This will, in turn, provide healthier plants and better production.

8. The problem of pests is something that cannot be entirely avoided when it comes to gardening. Making use of the raised bed garden hinders pests from getting through to your plants because the beds are positioned above the ground and pests can't jump from plant to plant like they do in a traditional garden. The box helps in creating a barrier,

thereby making it difficult for the pests to operate.

9.   The use of the raised beds garden protects bulb plants from being feasted upon by squirrels or birds and even from bugs and larger pests.

10.   The better aeration and non-compaction of the soil provided by the raised beds help the roots in spreading out more easily.

11.   The raised beds work fine for an area where there is a limited growing season. This is because the soil used for raised beds is not part of the ground which enables them to thaw faster when compared to a traditional garden. This allows you to plant earlier compared to planting into the ground directly.

12.   The raised beds make your garden neater and visibly appealing. They can be made with sitting areas on the sides as well to make it easy to perform most of your farming activity.

13.   The use of a raised bed garden provides you with more options in terms of how large or small you want them to be. This is not possible with traditional gardens because creating the desired plot size can be quite difficult. As for

the raised bed garden, you have more flexibility to build your garden based on your taste.

14.   The raised beds are comfortable physically and logistically. There is less room for weeds to grow and less time required to protect your garden from unwanted weeds.

What You Should Know Before Starting a Raised Bed Garden

Again, raised bed gardening is simply piled-up soil in an enclosed or confined space that may be made of wood, sturdy plastic, blocks, bricks, and so on situated in a sunny area. If you wish, you could build your own raised bed gardening without the frames and mound the soil high enough; say six to eight inches tall. The essential thing here is to flatten the top of the mounded soil and your choice's quality soil.

It makes gardening easier and brings it closer to home. Now, starting a raised bed garden is simple but not to be taken for granted. If you want to be successful at raised bed gardening, you should not take the concept for granted. It needs attention and commitment. Before you dive straight into raised bed gardening, it will do you a whole lot of good to know these points explained below before you embark on this journey.

1. **Be prepared**: Being prepared is the first step to starting your raised bed garden. It will do you a whole lot of good to be ready for it physically, mentally, and emotionally. If you don't feel prepared enough to start your garden, you will only pile up excuses after excuses which will transform into commitment issues for you. And when you have commitment issues, the garden takes a big blow for it, and a lousy beginning means an awful harvest, resulting in wastage of money, time, and energy. This might not be good for mental health, especially those starting their own raised bed gardens for therapeutic purposes.

2. **Another thing you should know is that raised bed gardening should not be taken for granted:** Yes, it seems fun and simple to create and build-up, but it should not be taken for granted because raised beds gardens also have the procedures and the guidelines they follow. The idea of it might seem simple, and you might want to lean on the "do it your way" processes. That is a bad idea because you should at least have the basic knowledge and the guidelines surrounding the ways of raised bed gardens. Doing it all wrong will only bring poor harvests and frustrations. It will be better to learn about it, understand the procedures and

how it works before starting your garden. Know the pros and cons of the type of bed you will later choose to create your own raised bed garden.

3. Know your capability and commitment level: When you know these, it will be easier to start a garden that is not more than what you can handle and nurture. Also, creating slow and small is the key to knowing these. When you start slow and small, as time goes on and you are now familiar with the whole concept of raised bed gardening, you will know if you are not satisfied with what you have built or if you are confident with what you have and then want to stop right there. When you know your level of commitment and handling, you will become relatively happier, and when you really want to go into raised bed gardening, it will be pretty easy for you.

4. Not much space is required to start your raised bed gardening: Don't get intimidated by the idea of starting your own raised bed garden and get frantic with worry about the space required for your raised beds. Raised bed gardens don't require much space, and you can have them in your own house. You need the basic requirements like the soil, the enclosed space of your choice you want for your soil to grow your crops on, and the essential equipment required in raised bed gardening.

5. Your raised beds' size and height: A remarkable thing about raised bed gardening is the choice you have in creating it all in your style: no pressure and no forced choosing. And knowing the size and the height you want your garden to have will make the raised bed gardening easier for you. Already said, raised bed gardens are usually three to four feet wide and about six to eight feet long. This gives space for easy reach into the raised beds and reduces the risk of condensing the soil. So, importantly, know the size and the height you want your raised beds to be. It is a matter of preference which might be affected by the cost of your choice of the raised bed, the required deepness, which depends on the intended crop to be grown, and also age and health-wise; the amount of the bending over you will have to do. So, for easy and enjoyable gardening, get familiar with the size and the height you want your raised bed to be.

6. Know the perfect spot for your raised bed garden: This will reduce the risk of confusion about where to start your garden. It will be easier to know the suitable area for you and your raised beds before beginning to prevent inconveniences at taking care of the garden later on. Your location doesn't have to be cliché. It doesn't necessarily have to be your backyard. It all depends on your preference, your taste and what you think suits you, and the purpose of starting your own raised bed garden. It could actually be your backyard or your front yard, your side yard, or anywhere suitable for you. It might even be your roof or your driveway! That is the sweet craziness that comes with raised bed gardens. It is not a blowout of proportion garden. It is your little world of nature, and knowing and picking out the perfect spot for you and your garden will help make the processes and experiences of building the garden enjoyable. In understanding the ideal place to choose for your raised bed garden, natural factors contributing to the increase and decrease in your crops' growth should be considered for a rewarding harvest.

7. **Know the amount of soil needed and what kind**: Seeking the help or the advice of an expert or an experienced person on this isn't far-fetched. Also, you could use some of the soil calculators out there, which can help you solve the issue of the amount of soil needed by determining the amount of soil required for the raised beds

for you. And when it comes to the quality of the soil to use, use the best quality which your pocket can support and garnish it with rich compost and manure.

8. Know the essential equipment required for raised bed gardening: Knowing the basic equipment used for raised bed gardening and how they work will speed your gardening experience and processes faster. Know and get familiar with the tools, features, and functions before you start your raised bed gardening. It will allow no space for frustration at what to use for what in the garden. And knowing the equipment and how and what they work for before starting the gardening will ensure a smooth and exciting gardening experience.

9. Know there will be weed and pest issues: Don't get bothered or freaked out by this. Weeds and pests are both unwanted elements in the life of crops. Though undesirable, they can be pretty persistent. But there are ways to control these unwanted visitors from your produce. You have it all under total control. The methods of controlling weed and pest control will be discussed later on in this book. It is good you know now and accept it is not all about throwing seeds into the soil. You water them, they germinate, and they grow, harvesting comes, and you reap it all. It doesn't work that way. Your crops will need tending and taking care of. This is why you should know your commitment and capability level before you start your raised bed gardening to prevent future wastage and poor harvests.

Armed with this knowledge, creating your own raised bed garden should be an easy and smooth running process.

CHAPTER 2: PLANNING YOUR RAISED BED GARDEN

By now, you have known and picked the spot you deemed suitable for your new raised bed garden. The next thing is to prepare the site you have selected in preparation for the rest of the processes that follow. You don't just clear a spot and start growing your crops. The site you have picked needs preparation, and after that comes the preparation of the soil you have decided to use in growing your crops. But first, let's get down to the preparation of the site.

Site Preparation

There are two basic methods that you can use in preparing the site for a raised bed garden. Both will be discussed, and you may choose the one which suits your style. Mark and identify the site you have chosen to use. You can drive short pegs to the ground or short sticks, use a rope or tape to join each driven peg or stick, and use it to mark the area and the length and breadth of the site so as not to exceed the length and breadth required. This will help reduce the risk of stepping on your soil when you are tending to the garden, compacting them.

The first one is the "No-Dig" method which Gardener Charles Dowding founded. And as the name implies, you don't have to dig through the ground of your site. Charles believes that when you dig weeds, it brings weed seeds to the soil's surface, and this just about creates more weeding for you to do in the future. When you dig, you have torn apart the fabric of your soil and the complexity that comes with it, decreasing its capability of withholding moisture and draining it. Also, Charles believes digging through the soil reduces the nutrients faster, and feeding the plants will have to happen frequently than you might want to. So, the "No-Dig" method is about weeding the surface of the ground of your site. You can use your hands to weed the grasses, mulch, or shallow hoeing. Also, you can make use of weed killers. You don't have to dig through the grounds. Debris here is raked up rather than dug in. This helps the soil retain its holding and draining of moisture prowess.

The "No-Dig" Method of Site Preparation for Raised Beds:

i.   Get rid of the weeds or grass as closer to the ground as possible, with any method you deem suitable. You can use your hands or the weed killer or simply mow them off.

ii. Cover the area with old newspaper or cardboard, this will rot down the soil, and any form of rope or tape which you have used in marking and measuring the site should be gotten rid of. Those won't decompose like cardboard or old newspapers.

iii. Make sure the old newspaper or cardboard are intersected; make sure each piece of cardboard or newspaper lay on another accordingly. Do not leave space for any of the weeds to slip through. Ensure the ground is covered by the cardboard or newspaper and are all overlapped at about six inches. This will ensure no weed is escaping through the cracks of the newspaper or cardboard.

iv. On top of the spread newspaper or cardboard, add your compost and manure. Make sure all are spread around the newspaper and cardboard.

The Digging Below the Ground Method:

The digging below the ground method in preparing a site is the opposite of the No-Dig process. It involves using a spade to dig up the soil to loosen it, rather than just clearing off the site's surface closer to the grounds:

Mark your chosen site; you can use a rope, tape, or a string to do so by tying them around short sticks or pegs that are driven into the ground. Also, a leveler can be used to ensure the ground's flatness using water running away from the area.

Get rid of the top layer with a shovel's deepness at about ten inches.

Get rid of all plant debris, rocks, stale roots, little stones.

Go a little further with the digging with a shovel to ensure the loosening of the soil. Just a few inches though, don't dig too deep.

Mix organic matter with the soil, such as compost or manure.

Soil Preparation

This is the step taken after your site preparation in readiness for the planting of your crops. Good soil equals good growth and bountiful harvests. When you have good soil to grow your vegetables on, your garden has a good head start and a solid foundation.

First things first, it will be of great benefit to a new gardener to be acquainted with the basic types of soil for gardening, their nutrient rates, moisture drainage and retaining capability, and how they do well in summer and winter. Below are the basic types of soil for gardening and their information required for the knowledge of gardening. It is up to the new gardener to choose the one they would love to grow their crops on, considering certain factors.

Types of Soil

The Silt Soil: this is a high fertility soil rating that is light and moisture retentive. It contains medium-sized particles that are well-drained and can retain water very well. The particles are easily condensed and are prone to be washing away by the rain due to the soil's delicate nature. With the addition of organic matter, the silt soil particles can be formed into better clumps that hold stability.

The Sandy Soil: sandy soils have a high water draining rate and are very easy to work with. During spring, they tend to get heated more than clay soils and are prone to drying out in the summer, and this leaves them with low nutrient rates, which are washed off by the rain. Organic matter as a solution helps boost the high water-retaining capacity and increases the plants' nutrients. This soil is light, airy, dry, and warm and tends to be acidic and low in nutrients.

The clay soil: this soil is a heavy type that enjoys high nutrients. In winter, this soil stays wet and cold, and in summer, cakes up; dry out. There are spaces in clay particles, and this helps the soil have the capacity of retaining a lot of water. Clay soils are composed of over twenty-five percent of clay. Because soil usually tends to hold a high amount of water, it drains water slowly, and it takes time to warm up to the summer heat. With the caking up and cracking of the clay soil, gardeners are usually put in trying times.

The loamy soil: this soil, also referred to as "the loam soil," is regarded the best in gardening. They strike a perfect balance in the soil particles and are seen as the gardeners' pride. Loam offers good drainage. It is very fertile, high in nutrients, and very easy to garden with. They are a combination of sandy, clay, and silt soil to prevent the negativity that comes from them. Though rich and fertile, the loamy soil still gains from the addition of organic matter.

Now that the types of soil have been discussed, by now, a new raised bed gardener should know the one he/she would love to use. Below are the easy steps for the soil preparation for a new raised bed gardener:

❖ **Get rid of plant debris, rocks, grass at the soil surface.** You can use a spade to dig up the grasses and divide the sods into little pieces of squares. Then, rake them off the planting area with the head or end of the spade.

❖ Since this is your first garden, **loosen the soil** and dig down a little further for the roots to get better access to the bottom ground.

❖ **Add a few inches of natural organic matter,** such as compost or old rich manure. It is a good start for your garden and gardening. After that, cover with mulch which will protect the soil from the winter season and conditions. The compost added will do an excellent job of protecting the soil in the winter also.

In the course of preparing your site and soil, it will be good to note that:

✓ The quality of the soil should be chosen according to taste, style, and pocket.

✓ The quantity of your soil will depend on the height of your raised bed garden. Don't raise your bed to the extent to which the required amount of soil to fill the bed with won't suit your pocket or budget.

✓ Be curious about the sources of the soil you want to purchase. It will prevent future damage and loss of crops.

✓ You should add natural organic matters as these are the best to use in starting your garden.

Recipe for the Raised Bed Soil

Please take note that this is for a 4-by-8 foot size of raised beds:

•   Four bags of topsoil (make sure the soil is free from pests and weeds before use).

•   Two bags of compost.

•   Two pails peat moss.

•   Shredded leaves or grass clippings (of 2-inch layer).

All these being thoroughly explored and discussed, on to the next level it is then!

CHAPTER 3: THE BASICS OF BUILDING YOUR OWN GARDEN BEDS

When it comes to getting a high-quality gardening soil that has good nutrients and allows you to plant more densely with more productivity, the raised bed garden is the thing for you. The way it is designed helps with an effective weed and pest management better than the traditional garden. It will also help in effective pain management because of the fact that it is raised and there will be less kneeling and bending to harvest or pick weeds.

Raised beds gardening can be started by anyone, even a total novice, using ready-to-assemble kits available for sales online or your self-created beds made of common tools. Here are the fundamentals of the placement stage to planting.

Choose a Good Location

Most plants need up to six to eight hours of exposure to

sunlight. It's a good thing to ensure that the long side of your raised bed faces the north-south while the rows should face the east-west side to give the beds more access to sunlight. It is advisable to avoid slopes and go for a plain location to make watering even, so you don't end up having a part waterlogged while the other part is cracked and dry.

You can decide whatever size and shape you want your raised beds to have, the most popular shape and size are the squares as well as small planters. It is advisable to keep the widths at four feet which is narrow enough to get into the center from both sides. You can also leave 18 inches to create space between the beds. Keeping two feet is good enough for the wheelbarrows, lawnmowers, and other similar garden tools. The height of the beds can be 1 to 2 feet, you can increase the height but just note that the higher the beds, the more the cost of maintenance.

Build a Long-lasting Garden Bed Frame

Building the raised beds is about being creative since they can be built from durable building materials such as concrete blocks, bricks, etc. Composite decking materials can be used as well. You can get materials from the Recycling and reuse centers; they have high-quality materials and affordable materials that can be used for small projects.

The most used materials for raised beds purposes is the lumber. It is very important to avoid using wood that is preserved with toxins since raised beds are usually used in growing edibles.

Make use of rot-resistant woods such as cedar, cypress, etc, though they are expensive unlike common woods like pine they do last longer. To assemble, you should make use of stainless steel or galvanized hardware. Also make use of bolts or screws as they are much easier to work with than the nails.

Get your Raised Garden Beds Assembled and Filled

Take a measurement of your site and ensure that it's large and leveled enough, it is also important to make sure your site is cleared from weeds and pests. You can employ the use of landscape fabric to help in stopping earthworms from getting into your garden as well as aerating the soil.

Get the raised beds assembled such that they can be easily moved anytime you want to. Like said earlier, make sure your raised beds are leveled. You can place wood mulch or gravel between the beds to provide a clean, dry, working space.

The raised garden bed soil should be made up of about 50% high-quality soil and 50% of the compost. Ensure you get 100% topsoil that is made up of organic matter and nutrients which your gardening will surely need for your garden.

Get Greenhouse Hoops to Cope with Longer Growing Seasons

The use of a simple framework of hoops along with a lightweight cover will help in coping better and longer in cool areas. It will also help in conserving moisture in the dry areas and protect your plants from insects. Make use of galvanized pipe straps in mounting a 1-inch PVC pipe into the bed walls. You can cut a half-inch flexible PVC tube which is 2 times long as the raised bed width. Then bend it and get it mounted to cover the place.

The use of polyethylene film will come in handy in raising the soil and help with air temperature during the early spring season. Nevertheless, you should regulate the temperature because I'm sure you don't want your plants baked. You need to avoid excessive heat from getting to your beds by removing the slit vents or cover when necessary.

The use of bed netting will come in handy in preventing pests from getting to your plants and at the same time still allows your plants to access air and light.

It is important to water your raised beds regularly and this can be done by hand or set up an automatic irrigation process.

The fundamentals of building your garden beds rest based on your knowledge of the types of building materials and the essential gardening tools and how they are used around the garden; each tool for its purpose. There are different types of building materials to choose from for your raised beds; it depends on your budget, preference, and taste.

Building Materials

The building materials are simply the common materials used in building or making up your raised beds; what the raised beds' buildings can be made of. The building materials also involve the tools used in putting these materials together, and each device may vary depending on the material you go for. Below are the popular and commonly used materials for building raised beds:

- **Wood**: Wood is the most used material in building raised beds. It is divided into treated and untreated. Treated woods have chemicals in them to prevent them from rotting. It is advised to line the beds' walls with polyethylene if you feel uncomfortable using treated woods. Untreated woods, on the other hand, though depending on the type, rot quickly. The best kind of wood to use is cedar. Cedar is the best wood for raised beds because they are rot-resistant. The presence of oils makes it insect-resistant and is very durable. Cedarwood can last ten-twenty years. Because of its high quality, cedarwood is very expensive.

- **Rock:** Rock is another excellent material for building raised beds, but this is best recommended when there are a lot of natural rocks around you, which of course, should be personal property. Though pretty difficult in building, the result is an indefinite one; it lasts long, one can daresay forever and requires little to no maintenance. Find a suitable method in holding the rocks together to get enough height on the walls. The rock option appears pocket-friendly when you have them ready to use without having to purchase. It can be a pretty expensive building material for your garden.

- **Bricks**: In using bricks, just like in rock, your budget should be considered because purchasing them can be pretty expensive too, although it depends on the type you want to buy; new or recycled. Bricks also have indefinite use and, once built, will house crops for years and years to come. Cheap alternatives are cinder blocks and cement blocks, which has increased in popularity in raised beds.

- **Galvanized metal/steel:** These are topping the popularity chart in raised beds. They don't rot out like wood, they are solid and sturdy, and these can be used for decades; they are damage resistant, and also, they are featured with low maintenance. They make perfect beds, and plants thrive well in them. You might want to consider your pocket capability if you prefer to bed your plants with galvanized metal/steel.

Gardening Materials

These are basic materials gardeners should have in the course of their garden. They all have the purpose they serve in all aspects of gardening processes:

The protective gears: These are gardening gloves, gardening boots, and a wide-brimmed hat. The gloves protect your hands from dirt, germs, and dangerous sharp objects like thorns and twigs. The gardening boots do the same protective job as the gardening gloves. The broad hat is recommended for the protection of the skin against the harsh rays of the sun. Also, the application of sunscreen is advised.

Water sources/tools: these could be a watering can, a hosepipe, or a sprinkler. It depends on your choice of watering your plants. Watering tools are used to feed the plants and the soil required amount of water; not too much and not less. Moisturizes the soil and helps the plants germinate healthily and quickly.

Rake: A rake is used for raking out unwanted debris on the soil's surface to prevent digging deep into the soil and risk damaging it. The waste is raked out and disposed of.

The diggers: These are: gardening fork, shovel, and spade. A shovel is used to dig and scoop out soil alongside the spade. Also, a spade can be used to cut off stubborn roots and are excellent for transplanting and also planting. The garden fork helps break up clumps of soil that are hard to deal with, paving the way for a fine soil texture for young plants to grow their roots and thrive.

A wheelbarrow: A wheelbarrow is a miscellaneous tool that is mainly used for transporting whatever might give a gardener problem in doing. It saves time and energy.

Trowel: A trowel is a planting tool used in transplanting or planting seedlings. It can also serve the purpose of digging out stubborn weeds and small chunks of soil for planting.

Shears: These are for pruning the plants and also used for clipping off unwanted buds or an unwanted growing part of a plant. Also, it can be used to tidy up the look of one's plants, especially flowers.

Note that these are the essential equipment and tools. There are still many others you may find crucial and required for you. It all boils down to your needs and wants concerning your using them.

How to Build Your Own Raised Bed Garden

This is about summing up all the step-by-step processes and discussions which have been going on so far, and this will bring you as a new raised bed gardener into the next level, which is planting. Now, let us go over how to build your own raised bed garden in a single, straight process without complexity.

For making your raised bed garden, the following should be ready:

✓ **Your prepared site**
✓ **Your prepared soil**: the types of soil you can use have been explained alongside their features and ups and downs. Also, simple soil preparation has been described.
✓ **Your gardening tools**; You can't start a garden with your kitchen utensil, can you? Get your gardening tools ready!
✓ **Your building material**, whichever you have decided to use, should be made ready and available.

Now, building your raised bed garden all about depends on the building materials you use. How the wood is built for raised beds is different from how the rock will be placed. Learn more about the material you choose to use and how they are placed and constructed for raised beds. The most popular and easily made raised bed is the four by four and the four by eight garden bed made from wood. To make the four by four raised bed:

i.   **Get your wood ready**; a four two by two wooden stakes or pegs and 2 by 12 boards which are two 8-foot long. Or you can get guidance about the size of stakes and boards you would use if you want something more than the four-by-four garden bed. Get them to cut the boards for you in half to make things easier and if you would love to do that on your own, have a saw ready.

ii. **Arrange/ build the frame**: With the boards on their edges, arrange the boards to form a square. These should have holes drilled in them already; this will prevent the wood from splitting. After that, the panels should be screwed at each corner. Then you assemble the bed.

iii. **Assemble the bed**: place the arranged bed frame onto the spot you want to use, which is your prepared site. Hammer down into the ground a 2x2 wooden stake on the inside of the frame in each corner, and fasten or attach each to the bed's structure to support the corners.

iv. **Fill the arranged bed with your prepared soil**, use your rake to level and smoothen it out and get ready to plant!

CHAPTER 4: WHAT TO PLANT IN YOUR RAISED BED GARDEN

By now, your raised beds are ready, and the issue of what to plant might occur if you have no idea of what to plant. That is why preparation is an essential requirement needed in planting. You should not be faced with the issue of what to grow just when you are ready to begin the planting. You should be armed with the knowledge of what you want to plant and go right through it after building your raised beds. What to plant in your raised bed garden is entirely determined by your choice. If you don't have particular plants to grow in mind, especially if you want to engage in raised bed gardening for therapeutic and healing purposes or just to shut out idleness. The following are the examples of what you can plant in your raised bed garden:

- ➤ Lettuce
- ➤ Tomatoes
- ➤ Carrots
- ➤ Lettuce

- Kale
- Leek
- Garlic
- Spinach
- Radish
- Beet
- Rose
- Marigold
- Thyme
- Rosemary
- Mint
- Parsley
- Basil
- Chive
- Sunflower
- Daffodils
- Daylilies
- Peas
- Beans

Vegetables to Grow on Raised beds

Root Vegetables

Root vegetables are plants fit for human consumption that grow underground. Examples are carrots, beets, radishes, potatoes, etc. They are suitable for raised beds and thrive in rock-free loose soil, which allows them space for spreading out.

How they are planted:

Root vegetables are considered cool-weather plants even though some prefer the hot weather, and are easy to grow, especially in raised beds which is actually considered the best for them to grow on. Adequate spacing is required for root vegetables. When the young seedlings are about three to four weeks old, they should be thinned out for appropriate spacing. You can do that by pulling them out or clipping them. Ensure the soil you want to use in planting them is rock-free and loose. Early spring and fall are the most appropriate time to plant root crops. Get your soil ready, sufficiently fertilize the soil and know the certain traits and qualities that come with each root vegetable.

While growing, some require steady water and while they have grown, some require a lot of water, you should also get familiar with their growing rates. Maturity begins early in some root vegetables than the others. After planting, thin them when they are three to four weeks old. Water them frequently and make sure you weed frequently too. They don't do well with weeds. Fertilizing is not much of an issue, it is not needed frequently and is mainly one to keep away pests.

Leafy greens

Examples of leafy greens are lettuce, spinach, kale, arugula, etc. simply put, they are the crops consumed as vegetables. These are nutritious and simple to grow in raised beds. If you are a lover of fresh, homemade salad, growing leafy greens are for you in your raised bed.

How they are planted:

They are considered to have shallow roots and they do not require tremendously rich soil. They however need plenty of sunshine and need to be watered constantly. Prepare the soil, and sow your greens' seeds as soon as they can be in early spring. Space them properly and make sure they are well covered by the soil and watered; you can install a suitable constant water supply for them. Do not allow space for weeds with them, you can mulch your garden for the prevention of weeds. Keep the soil rich by fertilizing it. You can make your own fertilizer; rich manure can be used as well as compost.

Tomatoes

In planting tomatoes in your raised beds, you are privileged to maintain the best condition for them during the progress of their planting. Tomatoes are an abundant source of vitamin C, potassium, folate, and vitamin K.

How they are planted:

Prepare your site which should be sunlight rich and your soil which should be a well-drained and a well fed organic one. If you prefer to start from growing the seeds, you should start that about six to eight weeks before the average last spring frost date. Then the seedlings are transplanted after the last spring frost. That time, the soil gets warm. Clip off the leaves at the foot of the plant and bury their roots about six inches than how they were before. They demand regular profound watering and feeding. Mulch up the foot of the plant to help retain moisture and when the fruits start peeking out, fertilize the base soil of the plants well. Support should be provided for your tomatoes as they grow. You could stake, cage, or fence them.

Onions, leeks, and garlic

Growing these in your raised bed garden is also a good idea. They can be planted together; they share the exact soil requirements. These vegetables have more benefits to them than just to spice up your food than you can imagine.

How they are planted:

Normally, you plant onions in early spring. Your raised bed for planting the onions should be at least four inches high and the spot should be where the onions will receive a lot of sunlight. Your prepared soil should be loose and well drained, also endowed with nitrogen, compost or manure. Place the onions chosen for planting in the ready holes and cover up with soil and water well. Leeks are planted like onions, only they don't have bulbs, seeds are started indoors and transplanted out in early spring. They are shallow-rooted and require a lot of water. Garlics and onions are families, they have a related growing methods and conditions, no surprise there.

Peas and beans

In raised bed gardening, peas and beans make a good team, as they surge the accessibility of nitrogen in the soil. They do well with moist soil on an adequate level and don't need to be profoundly adjusted with fertilizer. They are also highly nutritious. Rich in vitamin C, E, zinc, and protein, respectively.

How they are planted:

These vegetables love the sun and a well-drained soil. When you plant peas in raised beds, it prevents the seeds from getting sodden as they grow in cool spring weather. This warms the soil for the beans which are planted later. They do well with moist soil and don't need to be adjusted with too much fertilizer. The soil should be prepared with organic materials; compost or manure. When planting, proper spacing is required and support should be provided.

Growing Herbs on Raised Beds

Commonly, herbs are flavorful or sweet-smelling plants used in culinary aspects; flavoring and garnishing food, the medicinal aspects, and healing purposes. Plenty of organic matter should be used for them as they do better in well-drained soil. The best type of soil for growing herbs is a broad mix of compost and a neutral acidity rate. Example of herbs:

- Thyme
- Rosemary
- Basil
- Chives
- Dill
- Parsley
- Tarragon
- Sage
- Oregano
- Mint: these should not be planted with other popular herbs like thyme, rosemary, etc. they can be annoyingly invasive and only do well in dry-down soil and sunny spots.

A moderate depth for growing raised bed herbs is three to twelve inches, depending on the type of herb, and the material should be durable, sturdy, and, if you wish, pretty. If you plan to venture into herb growing in your raised bed, it will be good if you know more about the types of herbs, their soil requirement, and the ones that can be planted together or not. You don't want to make the mistake of combining two herbs that won't do well together or need different soil nutrient requirements.

Growing Flowers on Raised Beds

Flowers, even for a four-year-old, are known. They are mainly for aesthetic purposes and add a sweet-smelling aroma to one's environment. Flowers are some sort of planting companion which help pollinate one's crops faster because they attract pollinators such as bees and butterflies. Also, they help reduce the rate of pest infestation. And the presence of these pollinators hovering around your flowers adds to the beauty of the garden.

In growing flowers in raised beds, eight to twelve inches is the moderate depth. The best type of soil recommended in growing flowers is sandy loam soil, the perfect combination of sandy, clay, and silt soil and a measure of organic matter. There are two basic plant types in growing flowers in your raised bed garden: the annual and the perennial. The perennials are better plants because each year, they yield back on their own. The types of flowers to be produced depending on the gardener, be it annual or perennial ones. Note that many flowers can be planted on raised beds, just like the herbs. They all can't be explored. Also, they have different soil requirements and preferences. The new gardener is advised to look more into the type of flowers they would like to grow on their raised beds. Examples of flowers that can be planted on raised beds are:

- Daylilies
- Lavender
- Zinnia
- Sunflowers
- Marigold
- Impatiens
- Pansies
- Daffodils
- Morning glories
- Cosmos
- Blanket flower
- Roses, etc.

Again, it is required you do your research and make your decisions. There are lots of beautiful and colorful flowers out there to build on your raised bed to beautify your home and garden or whatever purpose it is planned for.

CHAPTER 5: PLANTING TECHNIQUES IN RAISED BEDS

Simply put, planting techniques in raised beds are ways or methods with which crops are grown to help manage the soil's life, manage a garden spot and help the soil retain its nutrients for a long time.

The basic and the common ones are:

> - Intercropping
> - Succession planting
> - Trap crops
> - Companion planting

Intercropping

Intercropping, also known as interplanting, is the growth of more than one crop in the same planting site at approximately the same time. If not, then almost the same time for specific valuable purposes. In raised beds, examples of plants that can be intercropped are:

- ✓ Onions, leeks, and garlic
- ✓ Onions, garlic, and tomatoes
- ✓ Broccoli, lettuce, and potatoes
- ✓ Marigolds, radishes, and cabbages
- ✓ Rosemary, carrots, and radishes
- ✓ Tomatoes, beets, and lettuce
- ✓ Lettuce, radishes, and turnips
- ✓ Radishes and cabbages
- ✓ Leeks and carrots, etc.

Advantages of Intercropping:

- ➤ To preserve space and time in growing more than one crop.
- ➤ Maintenance of soil fertility.
- ➤ To retain soil nutrients.
- ➤ To reduce insects and weeds.
- ➤ Decreases fertilizers application rate.
- ➤ Perfect use of soil's nutrient
- ➤ Bountiful harvests.

Disadvantages of Intercropping

- ➤ Reduced airflow.

- ➢ Problems with fungal diseases.
- ➢ If combinations of crops suitable and not suitable are not known or mastered, it can lead to low yields.
- ➢ For beginners, intercropping can be pretty complex and complicated.
- ➢ Pretty expensive.
- ➢ Time-consuming and attention-seeking. It might pose an issue for gardeners with commitment issues.

Succession Planting

Easily defined, succession planting is when a reigning crop has its heir to succeed it after harvest right on the same space or in the same season. And it goes on. Succession planting is also known as successive planting, is when two or more crops are planted in succession. When one harvest is reaped, another is sown in its stead; on the same ground.

Advantages of Succession Planting

- ➢ Soil fertility maintenance.

- To control weed, pests, and disease.
- A steady stream of income
- Through the growing season, succession planting helps gardeners take the full privilege of their garden spaces.
- Allows harvesting of crops for a more extended period.
- Waste prevention.
- Vegetables take advantage of warm soil and light levels.

Disadvantage of succession planting

The soil is overburdened and is not given a chance to recover from the previous planting. It can result in a decrease and loss of nutrients in the soil. To prevent the weakening of nutrients, modify the soil with organic materials such as compost or rich old manure and mulch in between planting and practice crop rotation.

Trap Crops

The ways with which a kid is distracted with cartoons and goodies to let their parents take their nap is how trap crops work in distracting pests away from the main crops. Another name for trap crop is the sacrificial crop; it sacrifices its well-being for the main crop to grow and flourish in peace. You grow trap crops intending to save your crops by luring away agricultural pests, especially insects. There are a lot of trap crops and their classifications, depending on the main crop. Examples of trap crops are:

➢ Radishes
➢ Corn
➢ Nasturtiums
➢ Nettles
➢ Chervil
➢ Sunflower
➢ Sudangrass
➢ Marigold

Advantages of Trap Crops

➢ To reduce the usage of pesticides.
➢ To reduce pesticide cost.
➢ Crops are harvested at their finest, in quality and quantity.
➢ Maintenance of the soil and the environment.
➢ Reserves indigenous natural enemies.

Disadvantages of Trap Crops

➤ It requires knowledge.

➤ Extra labor, materials, planning, and planting are involved.

➤ Trap crops are special sanctions to the insects, which may result in inefficiency of trap crops.

➤ Supervision of insects in trap crops is timely, and obligation issues will pose a problem.

Companion Planting

Companion planting is when different crops are planted in close proximity for various motives, could be for pollination, growth enhancements in yields, taking full advantage of space, pest control. The most famous example of the companion planting method is the "Three Sisters," commonly used by Native American farming societies. The "Three Sisters" are corn, pole beans, and squash with relative mutual benefit to each. Note that there are crops that can be in proximity while some cannot. It will be better, especially as a new gardener, to look more into the right combinations of companion planting to avoid future wastage and loss.

Advantages of Companion Planting

- ➢ It improves the soil's quality and enhances its fertility.
- ➢ Natural pest control.
- ➢ Aesthetic benefit.
- ➢ Natural Scaffolding; certain plants, when combined in planting, offer a support system to each other.
- ➢ Nurse Cropping; certain crops, when planted together, offer shades and protection to each other.

The Disadvantages of Companion Planting

It may get complicated and complex for someone who is not at the expertise level to know the exact types of plants to be combined for planting because not all plants are companionable.

However, combinations for companion planting is discussed in details in the next chapter.

CHAPTER 6: COMBINATIONS FOR COMPANION PLANTING

Companion planting idea involves taking two or more plant varieties that grow well together, planting them close together to get higher productivity making the plants healthier and stronger. A good understanding of this idea is that it's very useful in solving common gardening problems by working symbiotically to increase yields.

Research about the phenomenon has been conducted to determine the companion planting process and how two plants that grow this way are working together. They have been able to show that this system of planting works in the following ways.

i.   They have been able to help in protecting and shielding crops. The process makes room for delicate plants growing and benefiting from the presence of stronger varieties which helps in protecting them from the wind, sun or heavy rains when planted close by.

ii. The use of this concept also helps in improving the

process of pollination. Plants having flashy blooms or strong scents can attract insects that pollinate to plants in the same place to also benefit from the pollination process.

iii. Also, plant varieties that are known to draw pests away from the raised garden beds help in luring pests away from other plants thereby protecting the plants and trapping the pests.

iv. Some plants are known to also produce substances through their leaves and roots which help in repelling common pests that may be harmful to other plants.

v. Some plants are also known to produce essential nutrients into the soil while breaking down as well as fixing nitrogen from the atmosphere.

Apart from having the ability to increase productivity, engaging in the companion planting practice have other benefits which include:

❖ Improving flavor: In a situation where some aromatic herbs are planted with vegetables, they will help in improving the taste of such vegetables as well as improving their flavors.

❖ Reduced dependence on chemical pesticides: The companion planting is a way of integrated pest management which helps to get the pest controlled without having to use harmful chemicals on your raised bed garden.

❖ Increased biodiversity: The process of planning plant varieties together helps in the protection against monoculture by reducing the pests and disease impacts which preys on a single plant family. It also provides the enabling environment for the beneficial insects that are needed in the raised bed gardens.

For the fact that the raised garden beds practice is efficient, clean and easy, each group of plants is grown in a confined space thereby providing both opportunities and challenges. Having a good understanding of choosing the right bedfellows together for this space is a very important move in getting the best productivity from your crops.

Considerations in Companion Planting

To get started with companion plantings, few factors which might affect your raised garden beds must be put into consideration. These factors include:

i.   The kind of pests you are trying to address with this process.

ii.   The area in which your raised garden beds are located.

iii.   The nature of the soil used.

iv.   Weather conditions.

By understanding the problems that need to be solved goes a long way in helping to make the right decision about the right companion plants for your raised garden beds.

Companion Planting Favorites

1. Plants that attract pollinators

When working on your vegetable garden, especially if you're practicing the companion planting, it's advisable to plant crops that attract pollinators nearby or adjacent to your vegetable raised beds for high productivity.

Generally, flowering native plants are known to be attractive to pollinators due to their familiarities. So, it is advisable to include the growth of native plants because the insects may already recognize the local plants and thereby have a presence for such plants. To get started, you can find out the local plants that are recommended for your area from the local extension agents in your area. Afterward, you can go ahead with adding it with the following plant mix:

- Alyssum, Calendula, and Echinacea.

- Borage, Coriander, and Sage.

- Buckwheat, Cosmos, and Thyme.

- Agastache, Catmint, and Dill.

- Bee Balm, Clover, and Parsley.

2. Plants that repel pests and diseases

Some plants are known for producing compounds that can help in eliminating the growth and development of some organisms in the garden. The process of suppressing this organism is referred to as Allelopathy. The Marigold is a popular plant that is well known for this role; they have strong allelopathic properties which help in the reduction of harmful nematodes that may be present in the soil. For good results, it is advisable to grow marigolds first and till them into the soil before growing other plants.

Apart from Marigold, some plants do repel pests from feeding on your crops by producing unfavorable taste and smell. The following are the plants that can help repel pests along with the preferred crops to grow with them.

i. Potatoes: Catnip will help to repel Colorado potato beetles.

ii. Squash: Radishes will help in repelling a variety of pests. Gourds will help in repelling squash vine borers.

iii.   Tomatoes: Garlic, onions, and chives will help in preventing pests from munching the tomatoes. Asparagus helps in repelling tomato nematodes. Borage will repel tomato hornworm while Cilantro helps in deterring spider mites.

iv.   Cabbage, Kale, Broccoli: The Borage will help in deterring Cabbage moth caterpillars. Garlic uses its sulfur compounds in deterring a large number of pests. Nasturtiums that are planted in a nearby or adjacent bed will help in luring aphids away. Calendula is made up of a sticky substance that helps in attracting and capturing aphids while Marigold will help in deterring cabbage maggots.

v.   Carrots: Planting the Clover in a carrot bed will help in repelling wireworm. Lettuce, Basil, Nasturtium, and Tansy will help in repelling carrot rust fly.

vi.   Members of the Allium family which include leeks, onions, and garlic combined with some aromatic herbs such as rosemary, sage will help in repelling rust fly.

vii.   Asparagus: Basil, Calendula, Parsley, Tansy,

Nasturtium, and Tomatoes will help in repelling Asparagus beetles.

3. Planting combinations that improve flavor

This category is noted for its subjective nature and it is also a common companion planting practice for culinary herbs, medicinal herbs, and other plants. The following are the ideal companion plants that will work to improve flavors:

i.   Cilantro or Basil, when planted in a tomato bed, will improve flavor.

ii.   Borage, when planted with strawberries, is a mix that works for most home gardeners.

iii.   Chervil will improve the spiciness to radishes when they are both sown in the same raised garden bed.

iv.   Chamomile helps in the improvement of onion's flavor when they are both planted close together.

v.   Thyme planted close to strawberries will also help in improving flavors.

4. Plants that improve the soil nutrients

By adding peas, clover or beans to your raised garden beds will help in increasing the nitrogen content available in your soil. This is because these plants are known to store bacteria in their root nodules which help in extracting nitrogen from the atmosphere and afterward converting them into a useful form to the plants, the two plants combined as well as plants near them. By planting the following into a soil that lacks nitrogen will help in improving the nutrient in the soil:

i.   Bush beans

ii.   Chickpeas

iii.   Crimson clover or Dutch white.

iv.   Broad beans

v.   Snow, snap or shelling peas

vi.   Pole beans

The planting of buckwheat in raised garden beds also helps in adding calcium into the bed. When tomatoes are planted in bed a year before, it will result in a high concentration of calcium in such soil simply because tomatoes are naturally heavy feeders of calcium. It is advisable to plant root crops together to prevent them from competing for phosphorus.

5. Plants that provide shelter

Combining tall or vining plants as well as shade-loving plants will effectively work together to improve their growing conditions. The following combinations will work fine:

Broccoli with salad greens

The combination of these plants will help in shading spinach, lettuces, arugula as well as other greens as summer approaches. The large leaf that emanates from the broccoli plant expands to fill space; therefore, it is advisable to have them planted in alternating rows for optimal benefits.

Lettuces with peas

It is advisable to plant climbing peas on a trellis oriented east-west while on the north side of the trellis; you can have lettuce seeds planted there. At the early stage of the seasons when the peas are still young, the lettuce will be exposed to more sunshine and warm soil thereby speeding germination.

As soon as the peas are grown, the lettuce will then start to benefit from the shade they must have formed as summer begins to advance and more heat begins to show up. The combination of the lettuce and peas will help in extending the harvest of lettuce while also preventing premature bolting.

Companion Planting Practice to Avoid

In some situations, plants that are grown close may affect each other negatively. Such companion planting practices should be avoided and the plants include:

- Cucumbers with fragrant herbs

- Spinach and Potatoes

- Beets and pole beans

- Alliums families such as garlic with beans and peas

- Carrots with dill as well as other family members

Companion Planting Practice Recommended

Cabbage + Radishes + Marigolds

The planting combination of radishes with marigolds as well as cabbages helps in the control of cabbage maggots that usually attack the cabbage plant roots. In case you notice slug problems in your bed, it is advisable to add chives to help in solving these problems.

Tomatoes + Garlic/onions + Basil

The planting combination of garlic or onions along with tomatoes will help in repelling common pests including slug and snails action. When basil is planted in the same raised bed garden, it will help in enriching the flavor that the ripe tomatoes will produce.

Lettuce + Carrots + Chives

When lettuce is planted around carrots in the same raised bed garden, it will help in repelling carrot rust flies. The addition of the chives into the same bed the lettuce and carrots are grown will help in repelling aphids and flea beetles from killing the lettuce. In addition to this, they also help in repelling the carrot rust flies as well.

Squash + Runner beans + Corn

This is an old and popular practice of companion planting in which the three plants are grown together; all the three benefitting from each other. The Squash benefits from planting them together with corn and bean, and this will help in deterring common squash pests. The prickly squash vines are disliked by the raccoons, so they will leave the squash alone and once you have them grown with the corn, they will end up leaving the corn alone as well. The runner beans are also known to flower, thus attracting pollinating insects to your squash which is beneficial to them because squash needs this to bear fruits. The corn is also known to act as a natural trellis for vining beans.

Kale + Bush beans + Beets

In companion planting, it is important to put the soil levels which the plants will occupy into consideration. Beets are known to feed deeply in the garden unlike kale and beans that are known for their shallow roots and as a result, the competition level for nutrients will be different. They help in adding nutrients to the soil and tend to undergo harvesting earlier than the beets. As a gardener, it is important to avoid the planting of pole beans together with beets because they are incompatible.

In conclusion, it is important to take careful note of whichever pairing you choose to put into practice when trying out the companion planting throughout the season and how the crops react to the unique space and the garden beds specific conditions. This will help you to adjust and make corrections as well as knowing what will work for your high productivity to be achieved.

CHAPTER 7: RAISED BED GARDEN IDEAS

The Built-In Raised Beds

Raised beds gardening involves the growing of plants in soil that are at a higher level compared to the ground. This is carried out by making use of some type of frame or enclosure which is made from stone, wood, bales of hay or repurposed material such as old dresses. Depending on your choice, raised beds can be built from just simple materials; the cost of getting your raised beds on the track depends on how elaborate you want it to be but they are generally known to be less expensive when compared to the traditional gardens offering an enormous amount of benefits.

Depending on the gardener, the raised garden beds can be placed wherever you want them to be because they are movable, unlike traditional gardening. The crops produced from raised garden beds are usually healthier because it is easier to control the soil quality as well as water drainage. It also eliminates the stress that comes with bending and when built with enough space in between the beds, you can even sit down and work on your garden comfortably. It is common to have plants in a container on a patio included but you can incorporate a raised bed built in the structure of your patio incorporated using lumber or bricks. It will end up with a long-lasting location for perennial plants to be grown and mature.

Sunken Raised Bed

Instead of having to terrace the entire sloping yard area, you can have your garden created at an eye level. A stone patio can be used to create an alluring garden room which is surrounded by raised beds and perfect for sitting comfortably as well as relaxing with a view or sitting on the wall during gardening. This technique may involve the removal of a fair amount of soil and stonework but it lasts for a long time.

Colorful Concrete Block Garden

Amongst the many ways of building raised beds from recycled materials is the use of the concrete blocks which is very popular as well. Depending on the choice of the gardener, it can be painted to make it more beautiful. New blocks made out of concrete can be used and they are considered to be heavier than the older cinder blocks as such, they are very good for vegetable gardening.

Raised Bed Arbor

Gardening on an arbor or trellis in raised bed helps in making it easier to harvest vegetables and also keeping them clean unlike where they sprawl on the ground. Making use of vertical gardening gives the chance of growing more plants without having to take up more space. Either you make use of sprawling vegetables or flowering vines, the garden will create a living arbor which gives the vines plenty of exposure to sunshine without shading out the plants on the beds.

Trough Gardens

These techniques involve simply filling animal feeding troughs with good soil and then start up with the planting process with no assembling required. It is important to drill some drainage holes at the bottom of the garden before the soil is added. The metals help in giving the garden an industrial look and also helps in keeping the soil warm during the spring. Nevertheless, it is important to note that, based on whatever you decide to grow; extra water will be needed for your beds during the hottest period of the summertime.

Garage Doors Repurposed as a Garden

This is another very simple idea for raised garden beds. It's as easy as looking around the storage areas in your home or checking out a few salvage stores for items that are attractive and easy-to-put-together. Some gardeners even make use of vinyl garage doors which are connected to resin strengthened vinyl fence posts as well as finials. They are very attractive and require low maintenance without the need for painting or waterproofing and last much longer when compared to almost all wood products.

Custom Design Raised Beds for Your Space

The raised bed gardens are being designed such that they will fit up into any space. Making use of little creativity can help in creating an entire garden area of your choice. The gardener can build a multi-level raised bed set up in straight lines with the complete potting shed as well as night lighting. You can also create a bench section where you can sit like the one used in the front bed. As the plants start to fill in and the wood weathers, the garden will develop a natural and rustic appearance.

The Sheet Metal Raised Beds

The raised garden beds are also known to sit well at a level over the underground frost line which enables the soil to warm up faster during the spring season; as a result, planting can begin sooner. In a situation where you wish to make your soil toasty throughout summer, you can build the walls of your beds making use of metal similar to the sheet metal idea for raised beds. The metal will help in retaining all the heats coming from the sun. The sheet metal is easy to form into the shape of your choice and it's a great way of providing the heat needed to grow plants such as the Mediterranean plants like lavender and sage.

Milk Crate Garden

The milk crate garden can be structured into any shape of your choice and is known to be very portable. It is as easy as picking up a crate and placing it wherever you desire. This technique doesn't need drainage holes to be drilled and changing the soil is easy as well and can be done by just lifting the crate and dumping the soil in a compost pile.

Raised Bed Border

This is not a good option for yards that are made up of steep slopes but by building up the garden beds at the lowest sections of the gardens, you will create illusions of a level garden. It is therefore advisable to make your beds wide enough to have a layered flower garden with a border of shrubs which frames the back of the garden and creates plenty of room for the perennials which will provide your garden with textures, colors and also edge softening drapes.

Square Foot Raised Beds

The use of raised beds in growing vegetables enables gardeners to control the soil quality as well as preventing it from becoming compacted. Since vegetables, in general, can grow with no hindrances, the garden beds do not need to be high before you can benefit from growing them in the beds. As low as six to eight inches of the vegetable beds are enough to help improve their water drainage.

Hoop House Raised Bed

A multi-season vegetable garden can be created with the use of little pre-planning. Raised beds help in controlling the plants growing condition in your garden and also helps in keeping the vegetables safe from hungry animals in your area. By employing the hoop house technique in building your garden beds, you will be prepared for any weather conditions such as the spring and a formidable garden that will be able to withstand frost conditions.

Herb Spiral

The spiral gardens are popular permaculture techniques. They help in the increase in the amount of usable area of planting without them taking up more than a ground space in the garden. They can easily be built out of brick, stone, wood or just by mere piling up of soil. Their unusual shape, as well as the swirl of the plants, forms an eye-catching focal point in the garden. By employing the spiral shape in building your raised garden bed, all the plants will easily be at reach.

Defining a Space with Raised Beds

Gardening in small spaces will make the space cluttered and neglected but by carefully planning your garden and by putting the four-season structure into consideration, makes it more attractive and easy to manage. The beds can be created for any shape garden from pavers, bricks or composite decking material. They help in defining the space and make it look larger by breaking up the view and also creating an extra seating area in the shady part of the garden.

CHAPTER 8: THE ESSENTIAL ITEMS NEEDED TO START GROWING CROPS

The essential items needed to start growing your crops in your proposed or ready raised beds are no big deal. As long as you have your gardening materials ready, you are perfect to go. In growing crops on your raised bed garden, these are the basic and essential items needed:

Knowledge

You may want to ask about what knowledge is doing here. You don't want to venture into growing your crops without knowing crops and how they work? There is more to growing crops than just throwing seeds into the soil and waiting for them to germinate. First things first, be equipped with the knowledge of the crops you want to grow and ensure you are prepared and ready for growing your crops. From the planting techniques, you can see that plants work in different ways, and there are conditions in combining crops to produce. Know more about the crops you want to grow, how well they do in seasons, their nutrients requirement, and their combination with other crops.

Your Ready Raised Beds

It is obvious that growth cannot take place if there is no garden available? Therefore, your raised beds should be ready before you start growing crops. The ready-raised beds are essential to start growing your crops, since that is what will house the crops you want to grow. You must have prepared your site, your soil, your building materials must have been assembled and put in place, and the raised bed filled with the quality of soil you have chosen. Those are what make up ready-raised beds for growing your crops.

Your Gardening Tools

Gardening tools are essential to growing crops. As a beginner, you might be confused about the types of devices you should get for growing your crops. There are a lot of gardening tools for growing crops; some more essential than others. In the process of developing your crops or getting other tools, you might see some others that might catch your fancy and feel they are essential for you to use. The basic ones are:

1. **Your protective gears**: these include your gardening gloves, your garden boots, and a wide-brimmed hat or what you feel comfortable using in shielding your face from the harsh rays of the sun in severe weather conditions. As the name implies, protective gears protect you from harm that can cause injuries that can occur while growing — harms like getting pricked or stepping on sharp objects like thorns and twigs and getting sunburn.

2. **Trowel:** in growing crops, this is important. It can be used to dig up weeds and small holes and break up clumped-up soil. A trowel is also valuable for transplanting seedlings.

3. **Water sources**: to start growing your crops, you need to have your water source or sources ready. It might be a watering can. It might be automatic watering systems that include sprinklers, soaker hoses, and irrigation; drip irrigation is the best way to water one's raised beds. Water is vital to the life of the crops.

4. **Garden rake:** it is used to prepare a raised bed for planting, perfect for the leveling and spreading of soil on the raised beds and raking up debris and weeds closer to the ground level.

5. **Shovel, spade, garden fork:** Shovel and spade are used for digging and scooping out the soil. Also, a spade is a great item for cutting stubborn roots you might encounter while growing your crops. Also, it makes a good tool for transplanting and planting itself. A garden fork breaks up lumps of soil which might be giving you a difficult time and giving your soil a more pleasing texture for the crops you want to grow.

The Seed/Seedling

Seeds and seedlings can be used, depends on the situation, and depends on the gardener even though seeds are more economical. A seed is a start from the very scratch process, while a seedling is a seed that has sprouted. These are the essential items needed to start growing your crops.

Compost/fertilizer

Compost is formed by decomposing organic material. They can be leaves, twigs, animal manure, food wastes, grass clipping, eggshells, shells, etc. This is a pocket friendly fertilizer for farmers and is very rich in the nutrients required for the soil. It is an essential item needed to start growing your crops as they help the crops grow healthily and yield a lot when harvesting comes. Compost enables good soil structure, helps the soil hold nutrients, moisture and air. It maintains a neutral level of acidity in soil and keeps the crop disease free as they grow. The process by which compost is made by decomposing organic material is called composting. Fertilizers are soil and crops nutrients providers also, but they are mostly made from chemical substances; while compost is organic, fertilizer is inorganic. Both are essential to growing crops, without them, both the soil and the crops will have no sufficient nutrients and protection required for them.

Sunlight

In planning your raised bed garden, it is essential you choose a location where your crops will get sufficient sunlight. Which is why this is essential to growing your crops. Sunlight is an important factor which helps the crops grow and flourish well. At least, your crops need to get six to eight hours of sunlight to grow. It is mandatory you have a sunlight-ready spot for your crops when you want to start growing them because the rays of the sun will help your crops process carbon dioxide and water to make it their meal.

Best soil mixes

Soil mix is important for growing your crops because they can retain nutrients and moisture for the availability of the crops when they are in need of it. Thus, the crops won't need frequent watering and fertilizing. Soil mix is loose and well drained to prevent the decaying of the roots, the elements can soak up and steadily discharge water and nutrients. The basic ingredients for making your own best soil mix are: peat moss, perlite, vermiculite, fertilizers, and compost. You make your soil mix by thoroughly mixing these ingredients together, ensuring they are well mixed to achieve your desired result. As a new or prospective gardener, this is important for you as it makes growing your crops easier and smooth. Also, having great yields can be a very great bet for you.

The Secrets to a High Yielding Garden

The dream of all gardeners is to have a high-yielding garden that will result in generous harvests. Many gardeners, especially the new ones, just go through planting processes without taking care of the necessary procedures and items, and they get poor harvests at the end of it all. They see others doing well in their raised bed gardening, and they wonder how and what they have been doing wrong. The following are the secrets to a high yielding garden:

1. **Proper storage, organization, and protection of seeds and seedlings**: if these are not well protected, organized, or stored, it might have damaging effects on their growth later on. Healthy crops come from good seeds and seedlings, not damaged ones. Don't treat your seedlings and your seeds carelessly.

2. **The soil of good quality**: fertile soil with the right amount of required nutrients and qualities is important for

your crops' incredible growth. No plant will thrive in low-quality soil. The right soil texture, an adequate level of moisture, the correct rate of acidity, and rich organic matter are the soul of growing a good group, leading to a high-yielding garden and, in all, building up your soil to perfection.

3. **Regular weeding:** When consistency comes in, if one is not consistent enough in the garden's weeding, weeds will sprout up at alarming rates and take over your garden. Before you start planting, ensure you are sowing on a weed-free spot to prevent weeds from growing faster, which will prove to be strenuous.

4. **A balanced diet of soil and water:** feed your crops the adequate and required amount of sunshine and water. Too much of both can be bad for the crops and will bring forth poor yields.

5. **Perfect spacing**: this is important in the high-yielding garden. Planting the crops too close to each other restricts proper airflow, and too much space gives way for weeds to grow.

6. **Intercropping /succession planting:** both are known for their extra garden yields. If you want a yielding garden, practice these techniques of rowing crops. There will be an increase in your usual garden proceeds. But in intercropping, know the right combinations of the crop you would love to grow together. The wrong variety of crops can lead to a very poor harvest.

CHAPTER 9: TYPES OF RAISED BED GARDEN

There are 3 kinds of raised bed gardens: raised ground beds, containerized raised beds, and supported raised beds.

The Raised Ground Beds

The raised ground bed is the type of raised bed garden where the soil is not enclosed in a particular material or frame. It requires only the use of soil to build it. Gardeners who wish to grow crops in a large area but do not want the expenses that come with using frames used the raised ground beds. And it might not be due to the size of one's pocket. It might have to do with preference and choice. It is a flat-surfaced mound, commonly six to eight inches high. They keep pests away and reduce weed intrusion in crops, allowing proper root exploration in plants because of the loosened soil and enhanced soil drainage. If not correctly taken care of, the con to using a raised ground bed will wear away and sink back to the surrounding soil's expected level. Raised grounds beds are also called unframed raised beds.

The Supported Raised Beds

This is the opposite of the raised ground beds; they can also be called the framed raised beds. Supported raised beds have edges or frames that surround the beds in which the soil is enclosed. It might be wood, metal, bricks, plastics, etc., they are best fit for sloped and uneven yards, and also they add an alluring appeal to a garden. They share the same advantage with the raised ground beds; pest and weed control, better soil drainage, and proper stretching of root plants. Unlike the raised ground, supported raised beds let you throw in additional expenses for the frames and a large amount of soil is required to build them. The soil encountered difficulty retaining moisture during summer, especially the clay soil.

The Containerized Raised Beds

As the name implies, these raised beds are enclosed in containers. It might be pots, little plastic buckets, and many others. Gardeners can improvise and use containers of their choice so long it is appropriate for the soil and the plants to grow in. These are trim aesthetic materials that can be placed anywhere; window sills, offices, lawns, driveways. A containerized raised bed should have taller sides about ten inches or more. They require much soil to fill the containers, but their flexibility makes up for this. Containerized raised beds are easy to use and can serve more than one purpose for the owners; beauty, spice, and herbs can come in handy anywhere, anytime. These forms of raised beds need frequent watering and tending to; else, the plants dry off. Also, plants' growth may be restricted by the containers, and minimal amounts of plants can be grown there.

CHAPTER 10: PEST AND WEED CONTROL

Only plastic plants do not attract pests and weeds. It is natural and relatively normal for you to encounter issues with weeds and pests in your garden. The number one solution is commitment; be committed to your garden lest weeds and pests take total control of it in your absence. Lack of commitment is a sure ticket to loss, wastage of seeds, crops, time, and energy. As a new raised bed gardener, there is no need to feel intimidated about the issue of weeds and pests. It can only pose a real problem and danger for your crops when the situation has gotten out of hand. There are ways pests and weeds can be controlled and measured in your raised beds. Again, don't get daunted by this genuine concern.

Pest Control in a Raised Bed

Pest controls are the preventive measures taken to prevent pests from taking control over one's garden and damaging the crops, resulting in the extremely poor and low-quality harvest. If not totally controlled, they at least will be reduced to the most minimum level where they will hardly pose a threat and danger to your garden. The following are ways to control common pests in your gardens:

❖ **The use of garden-friendly insects:** not all insects threaten the well-being of your garden. These insects are also called beneficial insects. They feed on the pests, which are the actual danger to your garden. Be on the watch-out for these beneficial insects, and by luring them in with plants, they are attracted to. Examples of these insects are Spiders, Ground Beetles, Aphid Midges, Damsel Bugs, ladybugs, Braconid Wasps, etc.

❖ **Physical Barriers**: Use physical barriers to stop the pests from damaging your crops. The easiest and the simplest way to use physical barriers in pest control is using the net. This is done by positioning the net over the plants but still leaves enough space for the healthy growth of plants. A physical barrier's effectiveness depends on the type of plant you want to protect from a kind of pest. Don't mix up physical barriers for different pests and different plants. It might not work.

❖ **Grow high-quality plants:** when you take proper care of your seeds and seedlings, they produce healthy plants. The pests will attack an unhealthy plant and finish off the job of rendering it unproductive before they go for the healthy ones. They are not usually attracted to healthy plants like they are to poor growing plants. And growing high-quality plant stems from sowing healthy and good seedlings and having healthy soil. Before you raise your crops, ensure your soil is supplied with the essential and much-needed organic matter such as rich manure or compost for future pest control.

❖ **Employment of specific planting techniques:** you can control pests by practicing trap cropping, intercropping and companion planting. These crops significantly reduce pest infestation, especially the trap crops planted mainly for luring away nuisances from the garden's main crops. These planting techniques are done apart from the purpose of multiple harvests to protect one another, hence an excellent way of controlling pests.

❖ **The use of pesticides**: disease-carrying insects and pests can be controlled with the help of pesticides. Natural ways of controlling pests are better because pesticides can be hazardous. A little carelessness could result in many adverse effects. It could even result in death. Expertise level is demanded in the use of pesticides for pest control.

Examples of Pests; Animals and Insects

- Rats
- Mice
- Squirrels
- Rabbits
- Moths
- Bedbugs
- Fleas
- Blister Beetle
- Colorado Potato Beetle
- Mites
- Grasshoppers

- Striped Cucumber Beetle
- Aphids
- Cutworms
- Caterpillars, and many more others.

Weed Control in a Raised Bed

Weed control, same as pest control, is the preventive and control measures to disallow the overtaking of one's garden by weeds. In weeds, too, there are the bad guys and the good guys. Some weeds, just like the pests, are beneficial to the growth of the plants. Examples of valuable weeds are alliums, nettle, dandelion, wild mustard, and clover. Ways to control and prevent weeds in your garden:

1. **Consistency and commitment**: as a new gardener, it might want to take a while for you to ease yourself into the gardening process. Consistency and commitment do it. If you are not committed to your plants and consistent in your tending to them, it is only a matter of time before plants overpower your crops. Ease yourself into the art of gardening and be a good gardener. Don't let the weeds surface to an out-of-control level before you get rid of them. The result is a bad harvest as well as the hurt that comes with the wastage of money, time, and energy. To control and prevent weeds, be persistent in the care for your garden.

2. **Adequate spacing of plants**: when there is too much space between your crops, weeds find the opportunity to

grow efficiently. Don't plant too closely. Your crops need air and don't plant with too much space between your plants. That way, weeds can be controlled, and your plants receive unrestricted airflow.

3. **Drip Irrigation:** drip irrigation as the best watering method in raised beds proves its competency by supplying water only to the plants that need it.

4. **Regular weeding:** this works hand-in-hand with consistency and commitment. Regular weeding helps prevent and control weeds in your gardens. You can pull them out with their roots with your hands, dig them up with your spade. Get to each weed source, which is the root, and ensure that it is gotten rid of.

5. **Mulching:** it serves as a cover that suppresses weed growth by depriving them of sunlight and still retaining moisture. There are assortments of materials that can serve as the mulch. Examples are cardboard, newspaper, hay, leaves, manure, shells, leaves.

6. **Cover cropping**: you can prevent and control weeds by practicing cover cropping. These are grown for the purpose of them spreading out to cover the soil. They are crops that

grow while laying low and spreading out on the soil. They, among many other purposes, control the growth of weeds. Examples are peas, beans, rye, sweet potatoes, melons, pumpkins.

Fortified with these pest and weed control and preventive measure techniques. It is safe to say you will enjoy your garden and the process. Also, you will be rewarded with fresh, bountiful, and high-quality harvests!

CHAPTER 11: HARVESTING AND STORING YOUR CROPS

A major aspect of the raised bed gardening practice is being able to identify the right time to start harvesting your garden. Other factors need to be considered apart from when the crops are ripe – such as the length of the growing season as well as the effect of a frost.

Some vegetables such as cabbage, carrots, Brussels sprouts, kale, and parsnips will improve after frost and these make them sweeter. They can also stay for a longer period on the ground without having a negative effect. In the case of those plants that can't withstand cold, there are many ways available to help them in staying a little longer.

When such plants are faced with a light frost, you can have them protected overnight by making use of materials like row cover, older sheets, etc, to cover them up. This is usually worth the stress because the second frost that comes after the first one usually takes up to 2 – 3 weeks.

Taking the tomatoes for example, when there is early winter, they may not be ready for picking before the intense frost shows up. Once the intense frost is on its way, it's advisable to get out there and harvest all your tomatoes. There is nothing to be worried about especially for the green tomatoes that are up to three-fourth of their full size and already have some color elements because they will eventually ripen. You can as well have the tomatoes roots pulled up and have them get ripened gradually by positioning them upside down on the vine indoors.

Understanding When the Crops are Ready for Harvesting

When purchasing seed for your raised bed garden, you should take note of the days of maturity listed on the packet of the seed to give you a guideline in picking at the peak. Nevertheless, it is also important to put environmental conditions such as day length and temperatures into considerations as this also affects the period of harvest. If a crop is ripe, that doesn't mean it is necessarily ready to be harvested as different rules apply to different plants.

Examples are listed below:

i.   Onions and Potatoes: Harvest both the onions and potatoes when the top of the crops starts to die off or have fallen over.

ii.   Tomatoes and Apples: These fruits should be allowed to ripen on the plant. Nevertheless, some other fruits such as eggplant, snap beans, and squash are better picked when they are young.

iii.   Pepper: Whether ripe or not, they can be eaten at a size or state though they have more flavor when they are mature. At maturity, peppers are full-sized and must have turned into their final color.

iv.   Pumpkins: They shouldn't be harvested before maturities which are detected by performing thumbnail tests. When fully matured, the pumpkin will have a hard rind which will be able to resist puncture from the thumbnail.

v.   Crops such as the basil, lettuce, broccoli, and radishes which are grown for their vegetative parts such as the stems, roots, and leaves should be harvested when they are still young, tender and immature. For these crops, it is advisable to harvest early and more often.

These are just a few from the many crops available and it is important to note that the best time for harvesting is early in the morning as soon as the dew has dried up. The reason for this is that at this time the crops are still cool and will have crisper texture and more water content compared to when the weather is warm.

Useful Garden Tools for Harvesting

It is important to have a good understanding of the useful garden tools that will work well for harvesting to make the process easier for you. These useful garden tools include:

1. **Sharp Knife**: The sharp knife comes in handy for cutting vegetables like broccoli, cabbage, squash. This is a piece of essential harvest equipment that should be used.

2. **Gloves:** This should be worn before you start harvesting to protect your hands from thorns and brambles as well as crops that may harm the skin causing irritations. It is also advisable to wear a long

sleeve shirt to complement the gloves to make sure you are itch-free all through the harvesting process.

3. **Shears:** The pruning shear is the perfect equipment for harvesting crops that are made up of woody stems such as pumpkins, squash, peppers, etc.

4. **Spade**: The spade is very useful in harvesting root veggies. It is, however, important to be careful when digging because this can result in damaging or breaking your crops.

5. **Scissors**: These are very useful for cutting leafy vegetables as well as herbs.

6. **Hori Hori:** This is a common tool for landscaping for cutting woody stems as well as transplanting. They can also be used for mixing soil and many more.

Storing Your Crops

After successful harvesting, it is important to have a good understanding of how to store your crops effectively by considering the following requirements.

a. **Moisture**: It is important to note that vegetables that are stored are prone to shrivel quickly as well as losing their quality when there's no proper moisture. As a result, it is necessary to make sure that the storage area has humidity that is at about eighty to ninety percent relative humidity which is preferred by most vegetables. Making use of wet burlap bags, wet sphagnum moss layers, as well as moist sand, will help greatly in adding moisture.

b. **Temperature:** When the temperature is cool at about 32 to 55 degrees Fahrenheit, there will be reduced moisture loss and it will help in hindering bacteria growth and fungi that may damage the crops. In the case of green tomatoes, you can make the temperature warmer to help increase the rate of ripening.

c. **Ventilation:** Vegetables that have been harvested will still need oxygen for them to retain their high quality; therefore, you must make sure there is proper air circulation which will also help in minimizing wilting and tissue breakdown.

Another important factor to consider when storing your crops is having a good understanding of which storage conditions works best for the crop you are storing. Here are some of the things to consider:

i. Ensure refrigerating vegetables that have high water content as soon as they are harvested from your raised beds garden. Examples of these vegetables are cucumbers and carrots as well as the cabbage family.

ii. You can separate your vegetables into the storage groups for proper management. The storage groups include:

> Cool-dry for onion

> Dry for beans and peas

> Warm-dry for pumpkin and squash

> Cool-moist for potatoes and root crops

iii. It is important to note that crops like onions, potatoes, sweet potatoes, and winter squash do require a curing period to enhance the qualities of their storage.

iv. Crops such as the cabbage, cauliflower, leeks, kale, onions, Chinese cabbage, and beets should be stored under the mulch through fall frosts.

v. The Brussels sprouts can withstand light frost and they can be stored in the garden for months.

vi. You should avoid storing vegetables such as the onions, pumpkin, garlic, and winter squash inside the refrigerator. They are best stored in dark places that are at fifty to sixty degrees Fahrenheit with a normal humidity level.

vii. Root crops such as carrots, beets, potatoes, parsnips, and turnips can be left to grow for most of part of the winter period in the raised bed where they are grown. As soon as it is noticed that the ground begins to freeze, the vegetables can then be covered with hay, leaf and straw mulch to have them protected.

viii. It is essential to note that you should avoid storing some vegetables with apples simply because they release ethylene gas. This Ethylene gas ends up making the taste of the carrots bitter and they also reduce the storage life of pumpkins and Irish potatoes.

Canning

In the storing process, canning can be regarded as old-fashion but with the always evolving technology, better canning equipment is always coming up – this equipment is designed to safely preserve food supplies. By canning your crops you can be sure they will always stay fresh and ready to eat for you.

The canning method of storage works well for the healthy feeding of the family as well as keeping home-grown food secure. However, to engage in this method of storage, you have to consider perfect sanitation and also being attentive to details.

During the process of canning, it is advisable to take a good measurement of ingredients as well as monitoring air pressure and temperatures as well. To carry out the canning process effectively, it is important to take note of the following:

a) You have to be sure of the canning method to use. The two popular canning methods available are the pressure and water-bath canning. If you do not doubt your choice, it's advisable to make use of the pressure canner while some food will be safe using water-bath canning, especially in a situation where extra acid like the ascorbic and lemon juice is added.

b) It is important to make sure that both new and used jars are carefully inspected for cracks, chips or other small damage – if the jars are not in perfect state, they can leak out food and even break when under further pressure.

c) Take into detail the directions laid down by the manufacturer for the new pressure canner.

d) Make sure you stick to only recipes made available from trusted sources most especially those that are designed for canning. These recipes take the type, pH, size as well as other variables of what is stored in the can into consideration.

e) After filling up the can with whatever crops you are storing into it, be sure to give the pressure canner enough time to release air from the container via the petcock before the petcock is closed or before attaching a weighted gauge on it.

f) Canning at a height as low as two thousand feet will require you to add more boiling time as well as pressure.

Drying

Employing the process of drying when storing your crops, has more obvious advantages over the process of freezing and canning as well as other methods of preservation which usually require extreme temperatures. By making use of the process of drying to store your crops, you will be using less energy to store frozen foods compared to when they are stored via refrigeration and canning which usually require boiling. The following are other advantages that can be derived from the drying process:

❖ By drying your vegetables, they will weigh less and consume less space compared to when they are canned.

❖ They also have an added advantage of retaining

minerals and vitamins better than when frozen or canned.

❖ The vegetables will retain their fibers including flavor when they are preserved this way.

To carry out the drying process effectively, here are things you should always put into consideration.

❖ Drying at proper temperatures helps in retaining the natural enzymes present in the crop while also preventing enzymatic deterioration during the storage process.

❖ The gardener should make sure there is proper air circulation to allow heat and low humidity to carry out their part effectively.

❖ Keeping the temperatures around 140 degrees will help in drying most produce quickly as well as preserving its nutritional content.

❖ Avoid stacking or crowding vegetables as well as fruits you are drying so that the equipment used can effectively hold.

❖ Take note that a warmer and less humid condition makes drying faster.

❖ There is also a food dehydrator which is made up of a thermostat, heating elements, and blower which make the process of drying faster and under control.

Note that best storage results come from the best product, as a result, you should avoid making use of already bruised fruit or pepper that have overripe. Avoid storing bad produce in general since no form of preservation would make them better.

CHAPTER 12: ADVANTAGES AND DISADVANTAGES

Advantages of Raised Bed Gardening

• Accessibility for people who have health challenges such as bad backs because they can't always bend down to the ground, squat or bend over. Growing food in raised beds makes it easily accessible for them to work on their garden thereby erasing the stress and the back pains with other health challenges they may occur during the process.

• The raised bed gardening is known to look more attractive and easier to manage than the traditional garden system. It can be built with simple things like the cedar boxes, which can be placed in yards looking a lot nicer.

• They're not permanent. For example, if you live in an area where you don't want to dig in the ground, or you just can't, for instance if you're renting and the owners don't want you to dig or plant in the ground, then this is a great alternative because you can plant in the boxes and if you move you can just take the boxes apart, throw the dirt away and/or give the plant away and you're good to go.

• The ability to plant over bad soil is another perceived advantage. What I mean by bad is not a contaminated soil, that's another story in itself. By bad soil, I mean if you don't want to take the time to mulch it and create a good soil over some time but you want to plant right away, the raised beds can be placed over the top of the granite and fill it with compost and you will be ready to get started.

Disadvantages of Raised Bed Gardening

• It's more easily affected by heat and cold in other words, when you're growing in raised beds and you don't have a buffer zone, you don't have an insulation of dirt or soil around it; in the summertime the dirt, soil or compost will dry out a lot quicker thus you'll have to water a lot more. It will also heat up a lot more in the spring, sometimes that can be a benefit but for the most part, it's really hard to control the temperature and the water in a raised bed.

• Likewise in the wintertime, raised beds will be affected

more by the cold because you can't insulate them unless you've got the giant heating blanket that's 12 feet long that can be wrapped around it.

• It's harder to put a barrier around it, in other words like a fence or something like that or even if you just want to build up stones and rocks. Some people like to put fences around to keep the deer but they're very persistent so it's harder to put a border or a fence around it.

• You have to replace the material over time no matter what unless of course, you're using brick, cement blocks. Using this material even creates bigger challenges with lime leach in the summertime when it's 90 degrees outside; those bricks will get seriously hot and that creates another challenge in itself and If you're using wood, you're going to have to replace it over some time.

• Filling the beds with compost is another challenge being faced with raised bed gardening. What compost does over some time is that it settles in, and if you're going to have something permanent in there, for instance, grapes, it's going to just keep settling in and it's going to take the plants down with it as well.

- The challenge of replenishing it after the compost settles in and takes down the plant is another disadvantage as well.

CONCLUSION

It's been an exciting and enlightening journey all through. Starting from the basic knowledge about raised bed gardens to how they are built, their types, and what to plant in them. I hope this book has eased your fears and erased your doubts about owning your own raised bed garden and has shown you there is definitely nothing to be afraid of in starting your raised bed garden.

As a soon-to-be raised bed owner, know that consistency is the key, and commitment is the keychain to a successful harvest. It might be weird and awkward to ease your new garden into your old and probably tight schedules. You should know it is something you will definitely not regret starting. Starting a raised bed garden keeps you closer to nature, and in turn, you get rewarded with monetary values, lush and fresh food ingredients, and a soothing balm to a restless and wounded heart.

After your adventure with this book, I hope that even if you have not started planning to build your garden, you pay more reverence to Nature and use your knowledge for beneficial purposes. Knowledge and information like this shouldn't just be known, learned, and kept in your brainbox. You can be the reason why someone smiles by helping them get their own raised bed garden built or solve a problem related to it.

For whatever reason you have decided to take a seat through the ride of raised bed gardens, I wish you the very best in it. Glasses up plenty of monetary gains, more depth to your well of knowledge, and if you are venturing into raised bed gardening for the therapeutic purpose, I hope you find the healing and relief you need. Good luck with the starting of your garden!

OTHER BOOKS BY MARK B. CHASE

Hydroponics

http://getbook.at/hydroponicsbymarkchase

Psilocybin Mushrooms

http://getbook.at/psilocybinbymarkchase

Beekeeping for Beginners

http://getbook.at/beekeepingbymarkchase

Raising Chickens in Your Backyard

http://mybook.to/raisingchickenbymark

Printed in Great Britain
by Amazon

14470125R00079